1/15
355.5 Mon

LAKE PARK HIGH SCHOOL
ROSELLE, IL 60172

W

EXTREME SURVIVAL IN THE MILITARY

SURVIVING THE WORLD'S EXTREME REGIONS: DESERT, ARCTIC, MOUNTAINS, & JUNGLE

EXTREME SURVIVAL IN THE MILITARY

Learning Mental Endurance for Survival

Ropes & Knots for Survival

Survival at Sea

Survival Equipment

Survival First Aid

Survival in the Wilderness

Surviving by Trapping, Fishing, & Eating Plants

Surviving Captivity

Surviving Hostage Rescue Missions

Surviving Natural Disasters

Surviving the World's Extreme Regions:
Desert, Arctic, Mountains, & Jungle

Surviving with Navigation & Signaling

EXTREME SURVIVAL IN THE MILITARY

SURVIVING THE WORLD'S EXTREME REGIONS: DESERT, ARCTIC, MOUNTAINS, & JUNGLE

CHRIS McNAB

Introduction by Colonel John T. Carney. Jr., USAF-Ret.
President, Special Operations Warrior Foundation

MASON CREST

Mason Crest
450 Parkway Drive, Suite D
Broomall, PA 19008
www.masoncrest.com

Printed and bound in the United States of America.

10 9 8 7 6 5 4 3 2 1

Series ISBN: 978-1-4222-3081-7
ISBN: 978-1-4222-3092-3
ebook ISBN: 978-1-4222-8784-2

Cataloging-in-Publication Data on file with the Library of Congress.

Picture Credits
Corbis: 10, 18, 22, 24, 34, 56; **Military Picture Library:** 14; **TRH:** 6, 8, 20, 28, 32, 36, 39, 50, 52; **U.S. Department of Defense:** 38, 40.
Illustrations courtesy of Amber Books and De Agostini UK.

ACKNOWLEDGMENT
For authenticating this book, the Publishers would like to thank the Public Affairs Offices of the U.S. Special Operations Command, MacDill AFB, FL.; Army Special Operations Command, Fort Bragg, N.C.; Navy Special Warfare Command, Coronado, CA.; and the Air Force Special Operations Command, Hurlbert Field, FL.

IMPORTANT NOTICE
The survival techniques and information described in this publication are for educational use only. The publisher is not responsible for any direct, indirect, incidental or consequential damages as a result of the uses or misuses of the techniques and information within.

DEDICATION
This book is dedicated to those who perished in the terrorist attacks of September 11, 2001, and to the Special Forces soldiers who continually serve to defend freedom.

CONTENTS

KEY ICONS TO LOOK FOR:

Text-Dependent Questions: These questions send the reader back to the text for more careful attention to the evidence presented there.

Words to Understand: These words with their easy-to-understand definitions will increase the reader's understanding of the text, while building vocabulary skills.

Series Glossary of Key Terms: This back-of-the book glossary contains terminology used throughout this series. Words found here increase the reader's ability to read and comprehend higher-level books and articles in this field.

Research Projects: Readers are pointed toward areas of further inquiry connected to each chapter. Suggestions are provided for projects that encourage deeper research and analysis.

Sidebars: This boxed material within the main text allows readers to build knowledge, gain insights, explore possibilities, and broaden their perspectives by weaving together additional information to provide realistic and holistic perspectives.

INTRODUCTION

Elite forces are the tip of Freedom's spear. These small, special units are universally the first to engage, whether on reconnaissance missions into denied territory for larger, conventional forces or in direct action, surgical operations, preemptive strikes, retaliatory action, and hostage rescues. They lead the way in today's war on terrorism, the war on drugs, the war on transnational unrest, and in humanitarian operations as well as nation building. When large scale warfare erupts, they offer theater commanders a wide variety of unique, unconventional options.

Most such units are regionally oriented, acclimated to the culture and conversant in the languages of the areas where they operate. Since they deploy to those areas regularly, often for combined training exercises with indigenous forces, these elite units also serve as peacetime "global scouts" and "diplomacy multipliers," a beacon of hope for the democratic aspirations of oppressed peoples all over the globe.

Elite forces are truly "quiet professionals": their actions speak louder than words. They are self-motivated, self-confident, versatile, seasoned, mature individuals who rely on teamwork more than daring-do. Unfortunately, theirs is dangerous work. Since "Desert One"—the 1980 attempt to rescue hostages from the U.S. embassy in Tehran, for instance—American special operations forces have suffered casualties in real world operations at close to fifteen times the rate of U.S. conventional forces. By the very nature of the challenges which face special operations forces, training for these elite units has proven even more hazardous.

Thus it's with special pride that I join you in saluting the brave men and women who volunteer to serve in and support these magnificent units and who face such difficult challenges ahead.

Colonel John T. Carney, Jr., USAF-Ret.
President, Special Operations Warrior Foundation

To become an elite U.S. Army mountain soldier is not easy. In the U.S. Rangers alone, about 50 percent of recruits fail during training.

WORDS TO UNDERSTAND

dehydration: A dangerous condition where your body doesn't have enough water.

hypothermia: Another dangerous condition, this one caused by body temperatures dropping too low.

trench foot: A painful condition caused by the feet being wet too long that causes the skin to turn black and die.

frostbite: Injury caused by extreme cold; the nose, fingers, and toes are the parts of the body most likely to be frostbitten.

insulation: Material that prevents the loss of heat.

flexible: Easily bendable.

balaclava: A close-fitting hat that covers the whole head and neck except for parts of the face, usually made of wool.

SURVIVAL IN THE ARCTIC

The north polar region is a frozen ocean, the Arctic Ocean. The south polar region, or Antarctic continent, is a land mass which is extremely cold, and almost entirely covered by ice. This ice can be up to an amazing 15,000 feet (4.6 km) thick!

Both Antarctica and the Arctic have seasonal extremes of darkness and daylight. Generally speaking, the nights are long, even continuous, in winter. This can be a problem if you are a survivor because no heat is received directly from the sun, making the temperatures very cold. The annual mean temperature during the winter in Antarctica is -76°F (-60°C), and in the Arctic it is -40°F (-40°C).

Because of the tough polar environment, movement should be made only if you are in danger. The decision to travel when in a survival predicament should be based on the likelihood that you can reach safety before rescuers are able to find you, but be aware that the arctic air is very clear, making it difficult to estimate distances. Therefore, do not move if you are near a large object, like a crashed plane, as rescuers will be able to quickly locate you.

If you decide to leave camp, place a marker to show the rescue crews where you have gone. The snow-block shadow signal is the best signal in snow conditions. Simply build up snow in a large tall arrow flat on the ground. It should be as large as possible in an open area and should point exactly in the direction you intend to travel.

Soldiers of the Mountain and Artic Warfare Cadre, a specialized squad within the No. 3 Commando Brigade of the Royal Marines.

Try to follow running water if possible. That's because many communities live on a river or stream. Also, if you follow water, you will be able to replace the fluids you lose through exertion. There will be fish in the river or stream, and animals will be attracted to it to drink, giving you the opportunity to catch them. In addition, there will probably be many edible plants growing alongside it. However, don't build a raft and float on it. Many northern rivers are fast, cold, and dangerous, and can smash a raft into splinters.

If you decide to stay where you are and await rescue, it is very important that you get out of the wind. The combination of low temperatures and the wind creates a condition known as wind chill. This can pose great danger to the survivor: exposed flesh can freeze in seconds. This is why it is important to get

It is easy to be lost in the Arctic. The Arctic ice sheet surrounding the north pole is 670,000 square miles (1,740,000 sq km) in size.

into some sort of shelter very quickly. Do not try to battle with nature when building a shelter; work in harmony with it. In a polar region, you will most likely want to build a snow cave, snow trench, or igloo.

To make a snow shelter, you need a saw knife, snow knife, shovel, or machete to cut snow blocks. The snow from which you cut the blocks should be firm enough to support your weight.

When building shelters in snow and ice areas, the Royal Marines emphasize the following rules:

- Never lay a tool down in the snow; you will lose it.

- Never hurry; if you do, accidents and mistakes will happen.

- When building a shelter, drink as much water as possible because **dehydration** is a killer.

- Use as little energy as possible when building.

- Try to be as close as possible to the source of fuel for your fire.

- Take off clothes to keep cool during the physical activity of building. If you do not, your clothing will become soaked with sweat, and you will risk freezing.

- Always take time to plan where a shelter will be. For summer sheltering, remember that insects do not like wind, smoke, and plants such as yew.

- Always protect yourself from the cold and wet of the floor of your shelter with spruce boughs or some other form of insulation.

Don't forget the common principles about survival in shelters that will be covered in the mountain survival chapter (do not have more than one entrance, build a fire, etc.).

In the polar regions, fires are essential to survival. When trying to start a fire, remember to do so out of the wind or with your back to the wind. Always be sure that you have plenty of fuel supplies for your fire. Decide early on what type of fire you want. For example, if you build a log fire, you will have lots of warmth and light. However, it will burn quickly, and therefore it requires lots of fuel. In a snowy area, you could use up a lot of physical and mental energy by having to gather fresh firewood. Prepare your fire so that it burns for a long time. The most important thing is that you do not let your fire go out; keep it burning steadily.

The Marines give this advice on building a fire: Choose a sheltered site. Do not light a fire at the base of a stump or tree. Clear away all debris on the ground in a circle at least six feet (1.8 m) across until you reveal bare earth. If the ground is wet or covered with snow, build the fire on a platform constructed from green logs covered with a layer of earth or stones. In strong winds, dig a trench and light a fire in it. In windy conditions, encircle your fire with rocks. In the Arctic, a platform will be needed to prevent fire from melting down through deep snow and putting itself out.

If you can, build a fire reflector. This is a wall made out of logs or rocks that directs, or reflects, the heat where you want it. Do not build a fire up against a rock. Instead, put it so that you can sit between the rock and the fire. The rock will absorb heat from the fire and keep your back warm. However, you must remember that fire is always dangerous. Do not place wet rocks or stones near fires. Test rocks by banging them together. Do not use any that crack, sound hollow, or flake, and avoid slates and soft rocks. If rocks contain moisture, the moisture will expand faster than the rocks when heated, and the rocks may explode. If they do explode, they can fire off dangerous pieces of bulletlike stones.

MAKE CONNECTIONS: TIPS FOR SHELTERING

Here are some tips for finding shelter in freezing climates:

- Do not sleep on bare ground. Use insulating materials such as spruce or pine boughs, dry grass, dried moss, or leaves.
- Do not cut wood that is too big for your shelter; it uses valuable energy.
- Do not scatter your equipment on the ground. Keep it in one place to stop you losing it.
- Have a fire going while you are building a shelter. It can be used as a heat source, a morale booster, and can provide boiling water for a hot drink.

If you do not find shelter quickly, you could find yourself falling victim to a wide range of illnesses, including dehydration, **hypothermia**, **trench foot**, and **frostbite**. Other dangers of the polar regions include sunburn and carbon monoxide poisoning. Sunburn occurs due to rays of the sun reflecting upward from snow and ice. Carbon monoxide is a dangerous chemical that has no color or smell and is given off by any gas or stove. In extremely cold climates, shelters are likely to be small and well sealed against the elements. This means that carbon monoxide can build up to dangerous levels, potentially causing death.

The symptoms of carbon monoxide poisoning are difficult to detect, especially

A shelter protects from frostbite and hypothermia. This soldier dries out his gloves over a fire, which will help to keep him warm.

when they are happening to you. They include slight headache, dizziness, nausea, and perhaps vomiting. The victim may also suddenly fall unconscious. To treat, remove the patient to fresh air or a well-ventilated area and get him or her to breathe deeply. If unconscious, apply artificial respiration in a well-ventilated area. Give oxygen if available. When recovered, the patient should be allowed to rest and be given warm drinks. The patient should not undertake heavy work until fully recovered.

To prevent carbon monoxide poisoning, make sure that there are at least two ventilation holes in your shelter to let fresh air enter. Do not let fires burn up too high. Turn off all stoves and lamps before going to sleep.

In any survival situation, you must take food and water when and where you can find it. Do not wait. Fortunately there is plenty of water in the polar regions in the form of streams, lakes, ponds, snow, and ice. But remember: do not eat unmelted snow or ice. This lowers the body's temperature and can lead to various types of illnesses.

There are also many available types of food, both plant and animal. Lichen, a type of fungus that grows on rocks, has sustained many survivors in cold climates, but do not eat water hemlock, baneberry fruit, arctic buttercups, lupin, larkspur, locoweed, false hellebore, or death camas. They are all very poisonous.

A more important source of food is animals, though they can be difficult to catch. There are many animals that can provide a food source in snow and ice areas. Ones that should be avoided are wolves, bears, and walruses. These are very dangerous creatures, particularly if they are injured. There are other large animals like caribou, reindeer, and musk oxen. These provide plenty of food if caught, but without a gun a Marine probably won't attempt to kill them because of their antlers. Sheep can be found in many snowy regions. In the winter they go down to the valleys and lower areas, and they are an excellent source of food. The same is true of arctic hares, marmots, lemmings, ducks, geese, grouse, and seals. Always cook meat thoroughly, and do not eat the livers of seals or polar bears—they contain dangerous chemicals.

Along with food and shelter, your clothing and gear will help you to survive. The layer principle offers the maximum protection from your clothing. The principle is very simple: still air is the best form of **insulation**, and the best way of creating it is to trap it between layers of clothing. The more layers

RESEARCH PROJECT

This chapter provides a list of poisonous plants that may grow in a polar region. Use either the Internet or books to find out more about each of these plants. Draw or print off the Internet a picture of each plant listed. Beside each image, explain why it is poisonous and what it will do to a human body if it's eaten.

you wear, the greater the insulating effect. Next to the skin, wear thermal underwear. Over this, wear a woolen or wool mixture shirt. On top of this, wear a woolen or good fiber-pile sweater or jacket. The final layer must be windproof and waterproof. Use a fiber-pile down jacket with a covered zipper. This will prevent the wind and rain from entering, and will be a backup if the zipper fails. The jacket should have a deep hood big enough to cover a hat. It should also cover the lower part of the face for further protection. The sleeves should cover the hands, and the jacket should have wrist fasteners. It should also be big enough to go over several layers of clothing. The jacket should be knee-length and also have drawcords at the waist and hem. If you begin to sweat, loosen or remove some clothing. Try to keep clothing clean; dirt and grease clog the air spaces in your clothing and reduce insulation.

For any outdoor activity, it is best to equip yourself with a pair of waterproof boots. The best kind of footwear is walking boots with a **flexible** sole and a deep tread. Your boots should be big enough to let you wear two or three pairs of socks underneath. Socks that are too tight will restrict the blood circulation and the layer of warm air that is between them—this can lead to frozen feet.

TEXT-DEPENDENT QUESTIONS

1. Explain how to build a snow-block shadow signal.
2. Why you shouldn't build a raft to float on a polar stream?
3. Why you shouldn't you lay tools in snow when you're not using them?
4. Why is carbon monoxide a risk in polar regions?
5. What is the layer principle?

Always carry a spare pair of socks. Whenever your feet get wet, change your socks as quickly as possible to prevent sores.

Protecting your hands and head requires gloves and a hat. There are many woolen and ski gloves for sale, but mittens are warmer. However, they can be very clumsy if you want to use your fingers. Therefore, wear a thin pair of gloves over your mittens. If your hands get cold, place them inside your clothing under your armpits, next to your stomach, or between your thighs. Any sort of woolen hat or balaclava will help prevent heat loss, though of course they are not waterproof. Also, try to wear goggles; they will stop you from getting snow blindness.

Antarctica and the Arctic are two of the most dangerous places in the world because of their freezing temperatures. Remember: do not move unless it is absolutely necessary, and build a shelter using the guidelines from the Marines.

WORDS TO UNDERSTAND

density: **Thickness.**

fatigue: **Extreme tiredness.**

vulnerable: **Open to some injury.**

navigate: **Find one's way.**

priority: **What is most important.**

vegetation: **Plants.**

secure: **Prevent something from moving.**

conserving: **Using something carefully so it doesn't get used up.**

SURVIVAL IN THE DESERT

Deserts occupy around 20 percent of the Earth's land surface. As a general rule, deserts are hot during the day because there are few clouds to block the sunlight, but at night they become very cool when the ground releases all its heat into the air. Because of the low cloud density, the days are abnormally bright and the nights crystal clear. Deserts can also feature strong winds, and the lack of plants means that it is difficult to find shelter from the harsh sun.

Deserts have less than 10 inches (25 cm) of rainfall each year, and some deserts have no rain at all. The lack of moisture in the soil and in the atmosphere means that most of the sunlight bakes the ground and makes it impossible for humans to grow plants there. When rains do come to the desert, they are normally very hard. As a result, flash flooding (where normally dry streambeds are filled with huge amounts of water) is very common.

A special feature of the desert is mirages. These are the result of light being distorted when heated air rises from very hot sandy or stone surfaces. They usually occur when you are looking toward the sun, and they seem to make objects bend and ripple. A cruel effect of mirages in the desert is to often create the illusion of water, but as you get closer the water "disappears."

Soldiers trek across a desert. Sand deserts are the result of rocks being broken down by extreme heat and wind over millions of years.

French Legionnaires in Africa stop to consult their maps. All military maps are divided up into a grid, and the grid lines are numbered along the top and side of the map. These numbers are called coordinates.

Surprisingly, all deserts contain at least some manmade features, such as roads/trails, buildings, pipelines, and canals. As a survivor, you should look out for them: they may lead to civilization (though the distances may be great).

The French Legion's desert travel rules are as follows: avoid the midday sun; travel only in the evening, at night, or in the early morning. Do not walk aimlessly. Try to head for a coast, a road, a path, a water source, or an inhabited location. Keep in mind that objects in the desert always appear closer than they actually are. Therefore, multiply all your distance estimations by three. Try to follow trails. Avoid loose sand and rough terrain; they will cause **fatigue**. Winds in the desert can reach hurricane force, causing massive clouds of dust and sand known as sandstorms. These can be very dangerous. The eyes, ears, and nose are **vulnerable** to being filled by the swirling sand if they are not covered. In sandstorms, lie on your side with your back to the wind, then cover your face and sleep through the storm. (Don't worry—you won't get buried.) If possible, use a large rock or other landform to protect yourself.

Sandstorms can create total confusion. When the storm is over, all the landmarks you were using may be covered over entirely with sand. So when Elite soldiers see a storm coming, they mark their route with a tall object just as a stick or pole. When the storm is over, the stick shows them what direction they need to follow to continue their journey.

This is only one of many techniques that a survivor can use to **navigate** his way through a desert. Another method is to use the stars. The desert nights will normally be clear, which allows identification of the Southern Cross and the North Star.

You can also make your own maps. All you need is paper, something to write with, and a keen eye. First, find a high vantage point and look out over the

A well is essential for survival in the desert. At a temperature of 120° F (48° C) a human can, at best, live for only two days without water.

MAKE CONNECTIONS: THE CHANGING DESERT

The desert is constantly changing shape; it is never still. Hot strong winds blow sand dunes into new shapes, something which can make navigation difficult for the survivor. If you are traveling without a map, pick permanent features to travel toward—rocks, mountains, and trees are good examples. But beware, the shifting sands can cover objects many feet high, sand dunes might disappear overnight, and the whole landscape might change if there is a sand storm.

terrain in front of you. Then start to draw what you see in front of you as if you were looking straight down. Make a general map with blank patches, and then fill it in as you gain more information from other vantage points. Mark on your map anything that stands out—trees, strange rocks, hills, the direction of ridges, and riverbeds. You can also use your map to mark your traps and areas where food and fuel can be found. This can be very helpful to your fellow survivors.

As a survivor in the desert, your **priority** is to find water. Desert climates are very dangerous because you can lose more water through sweating than is available to drink. If this process goes too far, you can become dehydrated, and your blood becomes too thick to be pumped around your body by the heart. Once this happens, you can easily die.

A large cactus from the North American deserts can produce over two pints (1 liter) of drinkable, water-rich sap when cut open.

Legionnaires are taught to look for water underground. Find a dry lake or riverbed at its lowest part, and dig into the ground with a spade, stick, or rock. If you strike wet sand, stop digging at once and let the water seep in. However, if you do not have immediate success, stop digging and find another spot; you must save your energy.

The following are signs Legionnaires look for to find water:

- Swarming insects; watch particularly for bees or columns of ants.
- Lots of plants; **vegetation** is at its best when there is water nearby.
- Animals; grazing animals need water at dusk and dawn, though meat-eaters get liquid from their prey so they may not be heading for a water source.
- Large clumps of lush grass.
- Spring water seeping through rocks and mud.
- Birds; these might gather around water, but bear in mind that some birds fly long distances to get to water.

Water can also be found in moist sand or mud. Put the sand or mud into a cloth, and wring it out into a container. During the rainy season, make sure that as much water as possible is caught. The main types of plants that can give you a good drink are cacti, date palms, baobab trees, prickly pears, saxaul, and roots.

If you are lucky enough to find a pool of open water, beware. Some water in the desert can be poisonous, particularly lakes. Signs of poisonous water

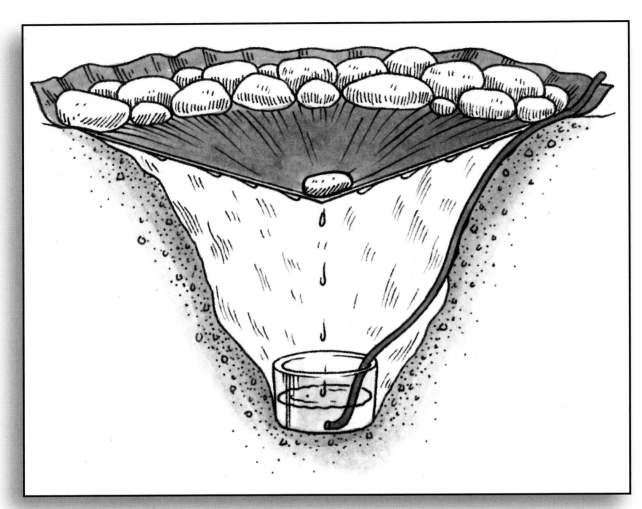

The solar still has a tube that runs down into a water container. The survivor can drink without having to take the still apart.

are: dead animals lying around; the water smells bad; foam or bubbles on the surface of the water; or there are no fresh and healthy plants nearby.

When you do find water, make it safe to drink by purifying it. The simplest way to do this is to first pour the water through a piece of cloth (this removes any large pieces of dirt), and then boil it over a fire for 10 minutes (boiling kills germs). After that, put in purification tablets. Water from plants, trees, shrubs, or dew rain will not need purifying.

Making a solar still is an effective way of catching water. You should dig a hole three feet across and two feet deep. Dig a drainage hole in the middle of the main hole, and put a container in it, then place a plastic sheet over the hole, and **secure** it with sand, dirt, or rocks. Place a rock in the center of the sheet. The sun raises the overall temperature of the air and soil in the hole to produce vapor. Water then condenses on the underside of the plastic sheet and runs down into the container.

Always keep in mind that water is more important than food. If you have food but little or no water, eat only small amounts until you find a fresh supply of water, because digesting food uses up large amounts of the body's fluids. If water is available, work out a sensible ration.

Along with water, clothing is extremely important for survival in the desert. Never throw away any clothing—you might need it later. Keep your head, legs, and body covered at all times. Do not roll up your sleeves; keep them rolled down and loose at the cuffs to protect your arms from the heat. Light-colored loose robes help to keep you cool and stop you from sweating too much.

Desert floors will be either intensely hot or intensely cold. This can cause the feet to blister and crack if they are not protected enough. The French Foreign Legion offers the following tips to avoid this: Do not attempt to walk barefoot, as it is unlikely that your feet will be hard enough for long distances. If you have shoes or boots, keep sand out of them by binding cloth, bandage, or other material over the top of the footwear, and around the ankle. Check

Soldiers always stay covered up in the desert. This keeps them cooler than letting their skin be exposed to the sun.

your footwear regularly and empty out any sand that is inside. Also, check for scorpions and other dangerous animals when putting on footwear, especially if you have taken off your boots overnight. If your footwear is a pair of weak shoes with thin soles, you can make them stronger by putting cloth inside the shoe or rubber on the sole itself. This will make the shoes stronger, and also stop some of the heat from getting to your feet.

The sun reflects its light and heat off the sand. This creates a blinding glare, which can make eyesight incredibly painful, and even send a soldier blind if he does not act quickly. Wear sunglasses or goggles if you have them. If not, a large piece of cloth can be wrapped around the face, leaving only small slits— look through these. Another Legion tip to reduce glare is smearing soot from a fire on the skin below the eyes.

Along with your clothes, shelter is necessary to protect yourself in the desert. Shelter protects you from heat during the day, and keeps you warm during the intense cold of the night. Build shelters during the early morning, late evening, or at night. Try to build a shelter near fuel (wood) and water if possible.

You should place the floor of the shelter about 18 inches above or below the desert surface to increase the cooling effect. The sides of the shelter should be movable to protect you during cold and windy periods, and to offer ventilation in the extreme heat. Keep in mind while building your shelter that there are many pesky insects in the desert. You do not want them around while you are sleeping, but they can be one of the easiest food sources in the desert.

Most desert animals—mammals, birds, reptiles, and insects—are edible. When looking for animals, keep an eye out for obvious signs such as droppings, tracks, trails, and feeding areas. You may have to lay traps for the larger animals and birds. However, keep a watch for owls, hawks, vultures, and foxes, which

TEXT-DEPENDENT QUESTIONS

1. How much of the Earth is desert land?
2. What are six signs that water is nearby?
3. List four ways you can tell if water is not safe to drink.
4. What are the steps to build a solar still?

often gather around freshly killed animals. You need the food just as much as them so chase them away, and take the meat for yourself. Always make sure that you cook the meat you have caught to prevent getting sick.

Plants are a good source of food. However you must be cautious because sharp thorns or spines can protect them, and there is always the danger they are poisonous. But they are not the only threat in the desert. Many insects are aggressive. Avoid ant nests. If you are bitten, put wet mud on the bite—this will soothe any redness, and reduce the pain. Centipede bites are painful and the effects can last up to two weeks. Scorpions stay under rocks during the day, and move around at night, often into sleeping bags or boots. Shake out your boots in the morning to check if there are any scorpions inside; their sting can be deadly. Spider bites are common in the wild. You may encounter black widows, fiddlebacks, and tarantulas in desert regions. Do your best to avoid them.

Much more serious than spider bites are bites from snakes. Venomous snakes found in desert areas include the cobra, viper, and rattlesnake. Your best

RESEARCH PROJECT

This chapter refers to the French Legionnaires. Find out more about this division of elite forces. Use the Internet as well as books from the library to answer these questions:

- When was the French Legion started?
- What are some major wars in which the Legion has fought?
- Who can enlist in the French Legion?
- Where is the French Legion fighting right now?

protection against snake bites is to wear protective clothing—most bites are below the knee or on the hand or forearm. Do not put your hands into places you cannot see and always wear boots. Be careful where you tread.

Animals are not the only source of danger in the desert. Dehydration can quickly kill even the strongest of soldiers. Heat cramps and heatstroke are two of the illnesses that are caused by dehydration.

There are many dangers in the desert, but if you follow the advice given by the French Foreign Legion, including finding and **conserving** water, building a shelter, and avoiding dangerous animals, you can survive in this dry climate.

WORDS TO UNDERSTAND

abound: Be plentiful; have a lot of something.

canopy: The upper layer of trees in a forest.

irritation: Soreness or itchiness.

circulation: Movement through something (as in the blood in the body).

SURVIVAL IN THE JUNGLE

The U.S. Army Special Forces (often referred to as the Green Berets) are familiar with tropical climates, which include rainforests, semi-evergreen seasonal forests, tropical scrub and thorn forests, and tropical savannas. The Green Berets don't have to know everything about these tropical jungles, but some information is vital.

Most important, they have to know what the climate will throw at them. Here is a quick check list:

- High temperatures and sweltering humidity.

- Heavy rainfall, which is often accompanied by thunder and lightning. This causes rivers to rise rapidly and turns them into raging torrents.

- Hurricanes, cyclones, and typhoons develop over sea areas and rush inland, resulting in tidal waves and devastation.

- There is a "dry" season (during which it only rains once a day) and a monsoon season (when it can rain for days or weeks continuously).

- Tropical day and night are of equal length.

Ideally, as a survivor in need of rescue, you should stay in one place. Food and water should not be a problem where you are; they usually **abound** in

Green Berets travel as light as possible in the jungle. They should not carry more than 30 pounds (14 kg) in weight.

In a dense jungle, smoke from a green-wood fire can be one of the best ways to let yourself be seen from the air.

the jungle. One of the best ways to make sure a rescue aircraft finds you is smoke. In daylight, smoke can be seen over long distances. Fires should be built, covered, and maintained, ready to be lit the very moment you hear a rescue aircraft's engines.

Fire is also very effective for signaling at night. Build a fire that gives out a lot of light using dry logs that burn quickly and brightly. A burning tree is a good way of attracting attention. Always try to select a tree well away from other trees—you do not want to start a forest fire!

Another Green Beret method of attracting attention is by using a reflector. On a sunny day, mirrors, polished metal cups, belt buckles, or other objects will reflect the sun's rays. You may have to climb a tree or a piece of high ground to make sure that you can be seen using the reflector.

However, the dense jungle **canopy** will make it difficult for any rescuers in planes or helicopters to see you or the signals you are sending. Travel may be the only realistic way of being found. Waterways offer the best travel routes. If you can, find a stream and travel downstream to a larger body of water. Though following a stream may mean crossing water and cutting through dense vegetation, a stream gives you a definite course that will probably lead to other human beings. It is also a source of food and water.

If you need to travel some distance, one of the best ways is to build a raft. Rafts should be used with great care, though. Some jungle waters are so fast they can destroy a raft and drown you in seconds.

When actually working your way through the jungle, a machete is one of the best aids for hacking down vegetation in your way. When using it, cut at a down and out angle, not flat and level: it requires less effort. While traveling, follow these rules from the Green Berets:

- Avoid thickets and swamps; move slowly and steadily through dense vegetation.
- Move through the jungle in daylight only.
- Use a stick to move vegetation to reduce the possibility of disturbing ant or scorpion nests with your hands or feet.
- Do not grab brush or vines to help you up slopes or over obstacles; their thorns and spines will cause **irritation** and they may not hold your weight.

A jungle patrol crosses a swamp. Swamps occur when water cannot drain away from the land because of poor drainage in the soil.

- Do not climb over logs if you can walk around them; you may slip and be injured or step on a snake.
- If using a trail, watch for disturbed areas—it may be a trap or pitfall.
- Do not follow a trail that has a rope barrier or grass net across it; it may lead to an animal trap.

Another danger you need to watch out for is quicksand. Quicksand is a mixture of sand and water. If you fall into it, you can get trapped and slowly drown. It is usually found near the mouths of large rivers and on flat shores. If you get caught in quicksand, adopt a spread-eagle position to help disperse your body weight and stop you from sinking. Spread out and swim or pull along the surface. Do not panic; you will sink faster if you do.

Keep in mind while you are moving throughout the jungle that animals are one of the biggest dangers. All animal bites are dangerous even if no poison is injected. This is because animal teeth contain lots of harmful bacteria. Once you are bitten, it is very likely that a wound will become seriously infected. If someone is bleeding heavily because an animal bit him, then you have to act quickly. The Green Berets have the following response to someone with a bleeding injury: Lay the victim down. Remove clothing around the place that is bleeding. Apply a forceful pressure directly over the bleeding with a large clean piece of material. In a real emergency, if you don't have this material, use your hand or fingers instead.

Keep the pressure constant until the bleeding is under control. This should happen in about 15 minutes. If the bleeding is from a limb, raise it high during treatment to reduce the amount of blood flowing there. Once the bleeding has stopped, leave the pad of material in place (unless it was very dirty to start with). Then bandage it (not too tightly) in place. Make sure you give the victim plenty to drink, but give only small sips at a time.

If a venomous animal bites someone, there is little you can do to stop the effect of the poison itself—once it is in, you cannot take it out. Your priority should be slowing down the **circulation** of the poison around the victim's body. Try to calm the victim as much as possible to slow the heartbeat. Wash the wound site with soap and water to remove any poison remaining on the surface. Then tie a tight bandage around the bitten limb (if a limb has been

An army survival instructor teaches U.S. troops how to deal with a cobra if encountered in the jungle.

bitten) above the place where the victim has been bitten. This should be tight, but not tight enough to cut off the blood flow.

Another type of poisoning occurs when poisons are placed onto the skin. This is often caused by brushing against plants that have poisonous thorns or leaves. The effect can be swollen, red skin, and a feeling that the skin is burning. The best way to treat this is to pour lots of fresh water over the wound to wash away the poison.

A different type of poisoning the Green Beret may have to treat occurs when someone has swallowed something poisonous. Many plants are very poisonous and will quickly make you sick. In this situation, your biggest decision is whether or not to make the person vomit. This can be good because it brings up the dangerous substance from the person's stomach rather than leaving it in there. However, it would be better if the person never ate the poisonous plant to begin with. When selecting which plants to eat, Green Berets have a list of general rules:

- Avoid plants with umbrella-shaped flowers, though carrots, celery, and parsley (all edible) are members of this family.

- Avoid all beans and peas.

- If in doubt, avoid all bulbs.

- Avoid all white and yellow berries—they are poisonous. Half of all red berries are poisonous. Blue or black berries are generally safe to eat.

- Single fruits on a stem are considered safe to eat.

- A milky sap indicates a poisonous plant.

- Plants that make your skin itch should not be eaten.

- Plants that grow in water or moist soil are often very tasty.

A soldier from the Royal Thai Air Force shows U.S. troops the edible portion of a banana tree during Search and Rescue and training.

If you are in doubt as to whether you can eat a plant, perform the Universal Edibility Test, used widely by the Special Forces. Test each element of a plant at a time by breaking it into separate parts: leaves, stems, and roots. Do not eat for eight hours before starting the test. During this fasting period, hold a

MAKE CONNECTIONS: A VARIETY OF WILDLIFE

Fortunately for the surviver, the tropics have an extremely rich wildlife population. Because of this, the Green Beret soldier should never go hungry in the jungle. There are literally millions of different species of plants and animals to be found. If you were to stand in the tropical rainforest for only ten minutes you might see a plant or creature that had never before been seen.

sample of the plant on the inside of your elbow or wrist. Wait 15 minutes to see if your skin reacts badly to the plant. (If it does, do not eat the plant.) Also, smell each component of the plant for strong or acidic odors—this is your first clue to edibility.

During the test period, do not eat or drink anything except pure water and the plant to be tested. Select a small portion of the plant. Before putting it in your mouth, put the plant piece on the outer surface of the lip to test for burning or itching. If, after three minutes, there is no reaction, place it on your tongue and hold for 15 minutes. If there is no reaction locally or elsewhere on your body, chew a piece thoroughly and hold it in your mouth for 15 minutes. Do not swallow. If there is no irritation during this time, swallow the food. Wait eight hours. If any ill effects occur, induce vomiting (by putting your fingers down your throat) and drink plenty of pure water. If

Bamboo can provide plenty of drinking water when it is split in half, as this Special Forces soldier demonstrates.

no bad effects occur, eat half a cup of the same plant prepared the same way. Wait another eight hours; if no ill effects are suffered, the plant as prepared is safe to eat.

Warning: Fungi should not be used in the taste test. Deadly fungi do not taste unpleasant and the symptoms of poisoning may not appear until several hours after eating. There is no antidote for fungal poisoning, so either know exactly what fungi are safe to eat or leave well alone.

A better source of food than plants is animals. They move along trails in the jungle, and that is where you should place your traps. The animals you can hope to trap are hedgehogs, porcupines, anteaters, mice, wild pigs, deer, wild cattle, squirrels, rats, and monkeys. Reptiles are abundant in the jungle and should be considered a food source. Avoid all brilliantly colored or strong-smelling frogs; they are poisonous. Treat all snakes with caution and kill them with a heavy blow to the back of the head.

If you are near a seashore, fish, crabs, lobsters, crayfish, and octopuses can be a part of your diet. Snails and limpets cling to rocks and seaweed above the low-water mark. Pry them off with a knife. Mussels form dense colonies in rock pools, on logs, or at the base of boulders. However, mussels are poisonous during the summer. The safest fish to eat are those from the open sea or deep water beyond the reef.

Streams are obviously your best source of water. If the stream is fast flowing with a stone and sand bed, it is likely to be pure, although you can't always be certain. Boil it for 10 minutes or put in purifying tablets if in doubt.

If there is not a stream around you, green bamboo often contains trapped water. Shake the bamboo; if a sloshing sound is heard water is present. Cut off the end of a section that has water in it and, if the water is clean, drink or pour from the open end. Coconuts also contain a refreshing liquid. The best coconuts to use are green, unripe, and about the size of a grapefruit.

There are many other ways to collect water in the jungle. One method is a vegetation still. Tie a clear plastic bag around a branch so that it covers the leaves at the end. Weigh or tie down the branch so that water from the leaves can drip into the bag as the sun warms it up.

Like food and water, shelter is necessary for survival in the jungle. The ground is damp and teeming with insects, leeches, and reptiles. You therefore do not

TEXT-DEPENDENT QUESTIONS

1. List some things you could use as reflectors for making a signal.
2. What should you do if you fall into quicksand?
3. Why are animal bites so dangerous?
4. Explain how to do the Universal Edibility Test.
5. How could you make a vegetation still?

want to sleep on it. (Snakes will be attracted to your body warmth during the night—you may wake up to find one curled around your stomach!) If you can, you should build a shelter on a high spot in a clearing well away from pools of water, where the ground will be drier, there will be fewer insects, and it will be easier to signal for help.

When clearing a site for a shelter, remember to clear away underbrush and dead vegetation. Crawling insects will not be able to approach as easily due to lack of cover, and snakes will be less likely to come toward you. Look above you when you have chosen your shelter site. You do not want to be below dead wood that comes crashing down in the next heavy wind, or a hornets' or wasps' nest.

Once you have made your shelter, you need somewhere to sleep. One of the best beds the Green Berets use is a hammock. A hammock can be made

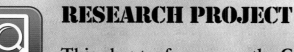

RESEARCH PROJECT

This chapter focuses on the Green Berets. Use books and the Internet to find out more about the Green Berets. Tell your class what you discover. Be sure to include the Green Berets' history, how they got their name, how they train, and where they are fighting right now.

quickly if you have a poncho or similar type of material and rope. A hammock may be tied between two or more trees for greater stability.

Always be on your guard in a tropical jungle. Some of the most dangerous plants and animals can be found here. If you follow the same guidelines as the Green Berets, though, you can be aware of these dangers and avoid them.

WORDS TO UNDERSTAND

elements: Weather conditions.

unpredictable: When you can't tell what will happen ahead of time.

summits: The tops of mountains.

pinnacles: High mountaintops.

casualties: People who have been injured.

harmony: Working with something instead of against it.

essential: Absolutely necessary.

synthetic: Manmade, not occurring naturally.

SURVIVAL IN THE MOUNTAINS

Mountains offer little protection from the elements. In fact, the climate you might experience on a mountain varies from place to place. However, there is one guiding rule—the higher you go, the colder it gets.

Mountain troops always get information about the weather before they set off into the mountains, and you should do the same. However, whatever the weather you expect, every soldier knows that mountain weather is an **unpredictable** thing, and they treat it with great respect. Storms can descend in seconds. Lightning is extremely dangerous on mountains because it is attracted to **summits** and **pinnacles**. Avoid these areas if a lightning storm occurs while you are on a mountain.

Other dangers to be aware of are rockslides and avalanches. There are several signs an elite soldier looks for to assess the possibility of avalanches. If the ground is hard and smooth, then snow is more likely to slide over it. Long grass will also provide a slippery surface for snow. If a slope is convex—meaning it bulges outward—it is more likely to have an avalanche. Also, the steeper the slope, the more likely the snow is to slide off it.

The U.S. Army gives the following advice for crossing avalanche danger areas. Cross a danger zone one at a time, connected by a rope. Cross the slope as high

A soldier uses an ice axe to climb an icy ridge. Some axes are so strong that they can take over 7,000 pounds (2,600 kg) of breaking strain.

as possible. Take advantage of any protection, such as rock outcrops. If an avalanche does begin and you are caught in it, remove your backpack and skis and try to run toward the side of an avalanche. Grab a tree or rock if possible. Sometimes you can "swim" in an avalanche. If swimming movements are possible, a double-action backstroke is the most effective, with your back to the force of the avalanche and the head up. Keep your mouth shut. In a powder snow avalanche, cover your mouth and nose with clothing to form an air space. Save your strength for when the avalanche loses momentum and settles. You must try to get to an air space near the surface; otherwise your chances of survival are minimal. Try to dig slowly to the surface and do not panic. Conserve oxygen by not shouting, which is unlikely to be heard anyway.

Elite forces are also trained in techniques for rescuing a teammate who has been caught in an avalanche. If you see someone taken by an avalanche, first mark the spot where you saw him or her before the avalanche fell, and then the place where the avalanche hit the person. Continue in a straight line beneath these two points to find the most likely place the person was buried. Then call for help, but do not leave the area to find assistance that is more than 15 minutes away—the victim might suffocate in that time. Look for anything like personal items that may show where the burial site is. Check the area by probing with an axe shaft or ski stick. If you find the victim, clear the mouth and nose of snow to help the person breathe. Remove the weight of snow from his chest.

Another emergency the U.S. Army is prepared for is if someone falls down a crevasse. Do not go too close to the edge to look down—you could end up joining the person. Pass a rope down with a loop in it. The person in the crevasse can put a foot in it and you can then haul them up. It usually takes

MAKE CONNECTIONS: CREVASSES

Crevasses are one of the greatest hazards of ice-covered mountains. Some of them are so deep that people have fallen down them and never been seen again despite many rescue attempts.

three strong people to haul an unconscious person out of a crevasse. But remember, speed is vital—temperatures in crevasses are absolutely freezing.

If you are a survivor on a mountain and are not going to be rescued quickly, you must get down into the valleys, toward civilization and away from the cold and wet. It is almost always better to use your time and energy to get down from a mountain than to dig a snow hole. Do not move in conditions, such as driving rain or whiteouts, where you can't see properly.

If there are a number of you, travel in single file. All mountain patrols tend to tie themselves together with ropes when moving through dangerous mountain conditions. The man-harness hitch, also called the butterfly knot, is good for tying together several people in a group. This will stop someone from getting lost during a blizzard, and if the first person falls into a crevasse, the rest of the team can quickly move backward and squat down with their heels dug into the snow to stop the fall.

When traveling up a snow slope, traversing (zigzagging) is much easier than going straight up. When traveling down a snow slope, you can make use of

A U.S. Ranger rappels down a cliff. The name "Rangers" comes from a band of U.S. troops who fought Native Americans in the 1700s.

the plunge step or step-by-step descending. Face the slope and lower yourself step by step, thrusting the toe of each boot into the snow while maintaining an anchor with an ice axe.

When you reach steeper sections of the mountain, use rope to ensure your safety. There are two varieties of rope: walking ropes and climbing ropes. A walking rope will break with a weight of 2,000 pounds (907 kg)—just enough to save a person on a fall, though not from a great height. That is why climbing ropes are essential. A rope intended to protect climbers against long drops should have a breaking strain of 4,200 pounds (1,900 kg).

All climbers depend on what are known as anchors. Anchors are points around which a rope can be tied. They will take the weight of a climber and also be strong enough to hold him on the rope if he falls. Many natural features, such as trees, can be used as anchor points. One of the best knots to use is the figure-eight loop, which can be tied at the end or in the middle of a line.

Two of the U.S. Army's climbing techniques are known as belaying and rappelling. Belaying is a way of climbing up a mountainside for two or more people with ropes. One person (the climber) ascends with a rope attached around the waist. The belayer anchors the rope around some solid feature with a loop tied in a figure-eight, and takes up any loose rope. The climber starts to climb, and the belayer keeps the rope tight to help the climber make the climb safely.

Rappelling helps a survivor with a rope descend quickly by sliding down a rope that has been tied around an anchor point above him. The climber faces the anchor point and straddles the rope. Then he pulls it from behind, takes it around either hip, diagonally across the chest, and back over the opposite shoulder. From there, the rope runs to the braking hand, which is on the same side of the hip that the rope crosses. You must lean with the braking hand down and be facing slightly sideways. Once mastered, rappelling lets you descend quickly and safely from high mountains.

While ascending or descending a mountainside, it is important that you are able to identify the following dangers:

- Wet or icy rock: can make an easy route impossible.

- Snow: may cover over useful holds or hide loose rocks.

- Smooth rock slabs: can be dangerous, especially if wet or icy.

- Rocks overgrown with moss or grass: treacherous when wet.

- Tufts of grass or small bushes: may be growing from loose soil that crumbles when touched.

- Rock falls: these are often caused by other climbers, heavy rain, and extreme temperature changes. In the event of a rock fall, find shelter fast, or, if this is not possible, press yourself into the slope to make yourself a smaller target.

While it is important and desirable for you to quickly get down to valleys and civilization, this is not always an option. One of your party may be injured; the most common first-aid situations are those involving broken bones and altitude sickness.

If you suspect someone of having a broken bone, perform the following actions. Remember that these procedures are intended only to help protect the injured limb until you can get the person to a hospital. Stop **casualties** from moving around. If the wound is bleeding, press down on it with a clean pad until the bleeding stops. In order to put pieces of bone into a straight line, perform traction. Traction is done by pulling a broken limb straight and then relaxing it back into the normal position. Please remember: this would not usually be done in a situation where rescue services are only minutes away. Only do it in a survival situation when you are days away from rescue, and it is only suitable for broken arms or legs. After traction is performed, keep the injured limb still through splinting.

An illness that occurs almost only on mountaintops is something called altitude sickness. This is very serious—it can kill even strong, healthy people. It is caused by the lack of oxygen in the air at high altitudes above 8,000 feet (2,400 m). There are two different types of altitude sickness, but all elite soldiers will know the symptoms to look for. These are:

Type 1

- Headache and feeling sick. Tiredness. Sleepiness. Dizziness.
- More acute head pain. Vomiting.
- The person starts staggering and becomes confused.
- Unconsciousness.

Type 2

- Harsh coughing.
- Difficult breathing.
- Severe problems with breathing.
- Unconsciousness and the breathing stops.

For a snow cave to be truly effective, the walls must be one foot (30 cm) thick, although the ceiling will sink a little as the weight settles.

If these symptoms occur, you should get the patient to a lower altitude. Be careful—the person is weak, so do not rush her or she may become more ill. When you are at a safe altitude, give the person plenty of rest and get them to professional medical help straight away.

If someone is injured or sick and you are unable to descend the mountain, you must do your best to make a shelter. This is not easy to do on a mountain because there are not a lot of materials besides rock, snow, and ice available. Do not try to battle with nature; work in **harmony** with it. For example, if there are trees, you can build shelters using logs and tree trunks. Snow caves may also offer shelter from cold weather.

Although there are different types of shelters that can be built in mountainous conditions, there are common principles that should be adhered to:

- Build a fire. Choose a fire that burns for a long time and requires minimum attention, and do not let it go out.

- Do not have more than one entrance. It is unnecessary and will cause your shelter to lose heat.

- Try to limit the number of trips you make outside and make the trips worthwhile—gather fuel and insulating material. To save yourself from going outside, dig connecting snow caves and use one as a bathroom.

- Never sit or sleep on the cold snow floor; always put thick insulation under yourself, even if you have a sleeping bag. Spruce or pine boughs give the most comfortable, dry sleeping area.

- Keep the inside of the shelter dry by brushing all snow off your clothes before entering.

TEXT-DEPENDENT QUESTIONS
1. Why is it so important to rescue someone from a crevasse as quickly as possible?
2. What is belaying?
3. What is rappelling?
4. List six dangers you might come across in the mountains.
5. What is altitude sickness?

- Remember to watch out for snow gathering on the roof of your shelter—it may cause the roof to collapse when it gets too heavy.

While building a fire and shelter is **essential** to survival in the mountains, the most important source of warmth is the clothing that you wear. Mountain troops follow what is known as the layering system. This means wearing many layers of clothing—each layer traps in air, which is warmed by the body. The first layer is known as the base layer. This is usually a thin layer of **synthetic** material, which transfers sweat from the skin away from the body. Next comes the insulating layer. The latest and most effective insulating material is fleece. Finally, there is the outer layer, also known as the "shell" layer. Ideally, this should be a breathable fabric jacket that has elasticized wrists and waistband, and a large hood to protect your face from the biting mountain winds. Boots are essential to protect your feet from conditions such as frostbite or trench foot.

RESEARCH PROJECT

This chapter mentions two kinds of knots: the man-harness hitch (also called the butterfly knot) and the figure-eight loop. Use either the Internet or books from the library to find out exactly how to make these knots. Draw diagrams that show each step. Do these knots have other uses besides those described in this chapter?

No matter how prepared you are, mountains are always dangerous. Weather is unpredictable, and storms can seem to appear out of nowhere. As a survivor, try to get down to civilization as quickly as possible, and keep in mind the guidelines laid out by the U.S. Army and other elite forces.

SERIES GLOSSARY OF KEY TERMS

camouflage: Something that makes it hard to distinguish someone or something from the terrain or landscape around them.

casualty: A person who is killed or injured in a war or accident.

covert: Done in secret.

dehydrated: When you don't have enough water in your body for it to function properly. Alternatively, dehydrated food is food that has had all the water removed so that it won't go bad.

dislocation: When a joint is separated; when a bone comes out of its socket.

edible: Able to be eaten.

exposure: A health condition that results from bad weather around you. For example, when you get hypothermia or frostbite from cold weather, these are the results of exposure.

flares: A device that burns brightly, and can be used to signal for help. They can only be used once.

hygiene: The techniques and practices involved with keeping yourself clean and healthy.

improvised: Used whatever was available to make or create something. When you don't have professionally made equipment, you can make improvised equipment from the materials naturally found around you.

insulation: Something that keeps you warm and protects you from the cold.

kit: All of the clothing and equipment carried by a soldier.

layering: A technique of dressing for the wilderness that involves wearing many layers of clothing. If you become too warm or too cold, it is easy to remove or add a layer.

marine: Having to do with the ocean.

morale: Confidence, enthusiasm, and discipline at any given time. When morale is high, you are emotionally prepared to do something difficult. When morale is low, you might be angry, scared, or anxious.

purification: The process of making water clean and safe enough to drink.

terrain: The physical features of a stretch of land. Hard or rough terrain might be mountains or thick forests, and easy terrain would be an open field.

windbreak: Something that you use to block the wind from hitting you. If you camp somewhere exposed to the wind, it will be very difficult to stay warm.

EQUIPMENT REQUIREMENTS

Desert

Hat with wide brim

Light-colored clothing (reflects
   sunlight)

Cloth neckpiece or scarf

Sunglasses or goggles

Walking boots

Medical pack

Sunblock

Plastic sheeting (to build shelters and
   make solar stills)

Sleeping bag

Survival knife

Water bottle and mug

Signaling mirror

Flint and steel firelighter

Jungle

Talcum powder

Insect repellent

Machete

Hammock

Mosquito netting

Tropical medicines

Walking boots

Spare shoelaces

Polar

Waterproof and windproof outer
   layers

Many inner layers of clothing for
   insulation

Snow goggles

Three layers of socks

Waterproof canvas boots

Ice axe

Ski stick

Rope

Face protector

Telescopic walking stick or ski stick

Compass

Mountains

Waterproof and windproof outer
   layers

Many inner layers of clothing for
   insulation

Goggles

Three layers of socks

Waterproof canvas boots

Ice axe

Ski stick

Safety helmet

Mountains (continued)

Woolen/thermal hat

Face protector

Walking boots

Ice axe

Sleeping bag

Tent

Foldable shovel

Binoculars

Carabiners

Climbing anchors

Climbing rope

USEFUL WEBSITES

To learn more about surviving in the world's most extreme regions, as well as the militaries that brave these harsh conditions regularly, visit the sites below:

www.10thmtndivassoc.org
www.desertusa.com/desert-activity/desert-survival-skills.html
www.goarmy.com
www.legion-recrute.com/en
www.mountainsurvival.com
www.wilderness-survival.net/chp13.php
www.wilderness-survival.net/chp14.php
www.wilderness-survival.net/mountain-survival

FURTHER READING

Borgenicht, David and Piven, Joshua. *The Complete Worst-Case Scenario Survival Handbook*. San Francisco, Calif.: Chronicle Books, 2007.

Johnson, Rich. *The Ultimate Survival Manual: 333 Skills That Will Get You Out Alive*. San Francisco, Calif.: Weldon Owen Inc., 2012.

McManners, Hugh. *The Complete Wilderness Training Manual*. New York: DK Publishing, 2007.

Van Tilburg, Christopher. *Emergency Survival: A Pocket Guide*. Seattle, Wash.: Mountaineers Books, 2001.

Wiseman, John. *SAS Survival Handbook, Revised Edition: For Any Climate, in Any Situation*. New York: William Morrow Paperbacks, 2009.

ABOUT THE AUTHOR

Dr. Chris McNab has written and edited numerous books on military history and elite forces survival. His publications to date include *German Paratroopers of World War II, The Illustrated History of the Vietnam War, First Aid Survival Manual*, and *Special Forces Endurance Techniques*, as well as many articles and features in other works. Forthcoming publications include books on the SAS, while Chris's wider research interests lie in literature and ancient history. Chris lives in South Wales, U.K.

INDEX

DATE DUE

PRINTED IN U.S.A.

LAKE PARK HIGH SCHOOL
ROSELLE, IL 60172